1. Remove hardware. Sand box and seal with matte finish. Paint or stain box.

2. Cover box with paper and images using PEELnSTICK adhesive.

3. Apply borders to the edges if desired. Cut narrow slashes on rounded corners.

4. Apply labels. Seal box, labels and borders with satin varnish.

5. Thread beads on the handle frame. Replace hinges, clasp and handle.

6. Attach accents, trims and decorations to the box with Goop Adhesive.

Celebrate friendships with the Good Friends label. A slide mount covered with a coordinating label shows off your best friends.

Good Friends

MATERIALS:
• *Darice* Purse parts (8¼" Square wood box, 2 Silver 1¼" handle clamps, Silver 6½" x 5" handle frame, Silver 1" clasp set, 2 Silver 10.5 mm corrugated rings, 34 Silver 10 mm melon beads)
• Cigar box labels (Good Friends, Buzzer, Crown Point Matches, 8 Black and Red cigar box borders) • *Design Originals* (#0454 Tiny Stars on Red paper, Large slide mount #0975) • Dark Blue cardstock
• *Jesse James* 1" Silver charms (1 flower, 4 hearts) • 2 Dark Blue 1½" tassels
• *DecoArt* (Burnt Umber acrylic paint, Satin water based varnish, Matte Clear acrylic sealer) • Adhesives

TIPS:

Painting: Thin Burnt Umber acrylic paint with water. Use a soft cloth to wipe paint on the sides, back and inside of box.

Slide Mount: Cut a slide mount in half. Center and glue the Buzzer label to the front section of the slide mount. Cut paper even with the edges of the mount. Cut paper from corner to corner forming an "X" in center of mount. Fold paper flaps toward back and glue to secure. Glue photo in mount. Mat mount on Dark Blue cardstock and glue to purse.

Heart buttons

Tassels with charm

Use an assortment of acrylic paints, adhesives and embellishments

Use box labels, strips, cigar band images and other papers

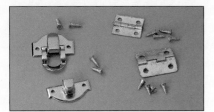

Silver and brass hinges and clasps

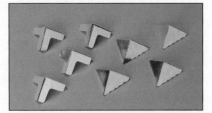

Silver and brass corners protect boxes from damage

Sequins, game pieces, charms and other embellishments

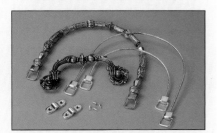

Silver and brass handle clamps and handle frames

Silk ribbon roses

Gold braid frame

Crystal rhinestones earrings

Gold filigree corner pieces

Reina Bella
"Beautiful Queen"

Give depth to an elegant image by adding as many dimensional touches as possible. Diamond earrings and other jewels accent her radiant beauty. Silk ribbon roses add realism to the image. Gold braid makes a frame fit for a queen while elegant filigree box corners complete this regal composition.

MATERIALS:
• *Darice* Purse parts (8¼" Square wood box, 2 Brass 1¼" handle clamps, Brass 6½" x 5" handle frame, Brass 1" clasp set, 4 Antique Gold 10.5 mm corrugated rings, 9 Antique Gold 25.5 x 11 mm faceted bicone beads, 10 Antique Gold 10 mm melon beads, 2 Crystal 4 mm rhinestones)
• Cigar box labels (Reina Bella, 8 Black and Red cigar box borders) • *Design Originals* Legacy Teal Stripe paper #0482
• 4 *Jesse James* Gold filigree corners • 2 *Offray* Red rose clusters • 30" of ⅜" Gold loop braid
• *DecoArt* (Yellow and Antique Gold acrylic paint, Satin water based varnish, Matte Clear acrylic sealer, Glazing medium)
• ¾" flat bottom stencil brush • Adhesives
TIPS:
Paint the sides, back and inside of box with Yellow. Let dry. • Mix equal parts of Gold paint and glazing medium. Dip a stencil brush in glaze and wipe excess on a paper towel. Randomly pounce the flat bottom of the brush up and down on the painted box leaving some Yellow showing.

Buzzer Butterfly

Enhance the labels and charms on this attractive box. Show off your art and stash your stuff for the next crop or sewing circle.

MATERIALS:
• *Darice* Purse parts (5¾" x 9¾" wood box, 2 Brass 1¼" handle clamps, Brass 6½" x 5" handle frame, Brass 1" clasp set, 8 Copper 28 x 17 mm oval spiral beads, 8 Copper 14 mm melon beads)
• Cigar box labels (Rofelda, Buzzer, 3 twins, Rosay Yo, EPCO and 3 matchboxes, 8 Gold and Red cigar box borders)
• *Jesse James* (5 Gold ¾" round buttons, 4 Gold ⅝" round buttons, 3 Light Amber hearts)
• *DecoArt* (Seafoam Blue and Seafoam Green acrylic paint, Satin water based varnish, Matte Clear acrylic sealer, Glazing medium) • ¾" flat bottom stencil brush • Adhesives
TIPS:
Paint sides, back and inside of box with Seafoam Green. Mix equal parts of Seafoam Blue and glazing medium. Dip brush in glaze and wipe excess on paper towel. Randomly pounce flat bottom of brush up and down on painted box, leaving some Seafoam Green showing.

Amber heart

Gold coin

Butterfly appliques

Sequin frame

Rhinestone jewels

Gold heart buttons

Butterflies

Carry a bit of summer with you year-round with this bright, sunny butterfly box. Get your theme started with these beautiful labels!

MATERIALS:
• *Darice* Purse parts (8¼" Square wood box, 2 Brass 1¼" handle clamps, Brass 6½" x 5" handle frame, Brass 1" clasp set, 4 Antique Gold 10.5 mm corrugated rings, 9 Antique Gold 25.5 x 11 mm faceted bicone beads, 10 Antique Gold 10 mm melon beads, 23 assorted rhinestones)
• Cigar box labels (Genuinos, Butterfly Safety Match, 8 Black and Red cigar box borders) *Hirschberg Schutz* Butterfly appliques (3" Orange, 1¼" Yellow) • 4 *Jesse James* Gold 1¼" heart buttons • 20" of Iridescent Blue sequins-by-the-yard
• *DecoArt* (Yellow and Antique Gold acrylic paint, Satin water based varnish, Matte Clear acrylic sealer, Glazing medium) • ¾" flat bottom stencil brush • Adhesives
TIPS:
Paint sides, back and inside of box with Yellow. Mix equal parts of Gold paint and glazing medium. Dip brush in glaze and wipe excess on paper towel. Randomly pounce flat bottom of brush up and down on painted box, leaving some Yellow showing.

Beaded handle

Nickel detail

Nickel corner flower

Bottle cap frame

Mother's or Grandmother's Purse

This Red Hat Lady is really brassy! Show off her family in bottle cap frames. Continue the metal theme with nickel charms and an eyelet quote. Notice the metal bicone beads in the purse handle.

MATERIALS:
• *Darice* Purse parts (7¼" Square wood box, 2 Silver 1¼" handle clamps, Silver 5½" x 3¾" handle frame, Silver 1" clasp set, 2 Silver 10.5 mm corrugated rings, 9 Silver bicone beads, 8 Green 10 mm beads)
• Cigar box labels (Lady in Red Hat, 8 Gold and Red cigar box borders) • *Design Originals* Legacy Green Floral paper #0480
• 6 Bottle caps
• *Making Memories* Nickel charms (4 raised flower corners, 1 eyelet quote)
• *DecoArt* (Green acrylic paint, Satin water based varnish, Matte Clear acrylic sealer, Glazing medium) • Adhesives

TIPS:
Mix even parts of Green acrylic paint and glazing medium. Use a soft cloth to wipe paint on sides, back and inside of box.

Cigar Bands - The number one collectible in the United States from 1890-1915 was cigar bands, but very few survive today. Many bands were decoupaged onto ashtrays, dishes and tables.

Dime Bank Cigar band circa 1940

Images of attractive women have always been used in ads meant to sell products to men. The cigar box labels of the 1870's pictured long-haired, full-faced women. The embossed lithographs made from 1890-1920 often featured romantic images and enticing females of various ethnicity.

Originally the **Cuban Heiress** label was embossed in gold, printed by Schlegel Litho, NY.

The **Rover** label originally dates from the beginning of the 20th century. The city of Amsterdam, NY, had 9 broom manufacturing plants flourishing from 1911 - WW II.

The original cigar box label of **Dick Custer** was circa 1920. A single label may sell for $25.00 or more.

Three Twins, circa 1930

Revenue Stamps - Between 1862 - 1932, revenue stamps were wrapped around cigar boxes as proof that tobacco taxes were paid. Once the box was opened and the stamp broken, it was against the law to refill the box for cigar sales.

The **White Persian Cat** was a favorite in the 1890's. The original White Cat label for a cigar box was printed by Consolidated Lithographing Corp. of Brooklyn, New York in 1911. Other charming kitty labels appeared in 1900.

In the 1850's, labels were plain, however some used single colors. In the 1860's and 1870's, multi-colored labels with bold, pictorial designs came into being.

The original **Good Friends** label designed for a cigar box was colorful and heavily embossed in metallic gold. It was printed by Krueger and Braun of NY, 1880-1898. It shows Columbia, personifying the United States, shaking hands with Lebertad de Cuba, the woman personifying Free Cuba.

History of Cigar Labels

Vintage Cigar Labels are a popular collectible today. Many of these beautiful images are framed to grace libraries, offices and homes. The appeal of these romantic images spans the world.

The first recorded documentation of the "holy herb" (tobacco) was written by Romano Pano, a Spanish monk who accompanied Christopher Columbus on his second voyage to America. Portuguese settlements in Brazil began cultivating tobacco for export to Lisbon in 1548. Jean Nicot, French ambassador to Portugal, introduced tobacco in France in 1556, and it is from his name that the word "nicotine" is derived. In 1566, Nicot sent snuff to Queen Catherine de Medici to treat her migraines. She called tobacco "Herba Regina".

In 1564, tobacco was brought to England by Sir John Hawkins. It was used primarily by sailors in Sir Francis Drake's fleet. Drake introduced Sir Walter Raleigh to pipe smoking in 1885, and Raleigh is credited with bringing it to the English court.[1] In 1586, a group of Virginia colonists created quite a stir at the Plymouth docks when they stepped ashore with their clay tobacco pipes.

Until the 1930's, cigar manufacturing was one of the wealthiest industries in the world and they spared no expense competing against one another with advertising art. Stone lithography was expensive, labor intensive and beautiful. The art used gold flake embossing, and many colors. The press used to produce this work weighed 43 tons.

Cigar labels are an important part of commercial art history. The label was the primary enticement for consumers to choose a specific brand. Since it follows that a good quality product comes in an attractive container, customers will most likely be drawn to the most opulently decorated boxes. Richly embellished and often embossed, these images represent the epitome of complex printmaking techniques and artistry.[2]

In the 1860's, cigar boxes were decorated on the side and lid, since they were stacked on shelves in shops; however, counter showcases were developed to display open boxes in the early 1870's. The visible inside box lid offered another opportunity to attract the customer with bold graphics and grand art.[3] Cigar boxes used intricate works of art on the lid, as a seal around the box, and under the lid. This tradition continues today.

1. Joe and Sue Davidson, Smokers Art, p. 10, The Wellfleet Press, 1997.
2. www.artoftheprint.com
3. Joe and Sue Davidson, Smokers Art, p. 208-209, The Wellfleet Press, 1997.

Simple metal corners and coins complement the brass handle and clasp on this purse. The background colors allow this beautiful image to stand as the focal point. The title means "the flower of the Bustillo family".

Lady with Coins

MATERIALS:
• *Darice* Purse parts (5⅜" x 8½" Wood box, 2 Brass 1¼" handle clamps, Brass 6½" x 5" handle frame, Brass 1" clasp set, 8 Brass corners, 12 Antique Gold 25.5 x11 mm faceted bicone beads, 11 Antique Gold 10.5 mm corrugated rings, 8 assorted Gold and Silver coins)
• Cigar box labels (Bustillo, 8 Gold and Red cigar box borders)
• *DecoArt* (Ivory and Burnt Umber acrylic paint, Satin water based varnish, Matte Clear acrylic sealer) • Adhesives
• Old toothbrush • Craft stick

TIPS:
Paint sides, back, front and inside of box with Ivory. Dip toothbrush in Burnt Umber paint thinned with water. Hold brush over box while drawing a craft stick across bristles.

Metal box corners

Metal coins

Decorative key

Metal bookplate

Lady and Keys

Decorate your treasure box with a beautiful label and keys. Turn it into a purse, and take your treasures with you. The sturdy beaded handle complements the colors in the purse.

MATERIALS:
• *Darice* Purse parts (7¼" Square wood box, 2 Silver 1¼" handle clamps, Silver 5½" x 3¾" handle frame, Silver 1" clasp set, 2 Silver 10.5 mm corrugated rings, 9 Silver bicone beads, 8 Green 10 mm beads)
• Cigar box labels (La Patura and matchbox labels, 8 Gold and Red cigar box borders)
• 4 *Making Memories* nickel raised flower corners • *Li'l Davis Designs* (2 keys, 1 bookplate, 2 Silver brads)
• *DecoArt* (Green acrylic paint, Satin water based varnish, Matte Clear acrylic sealer, Glazing medium) • Adhesives
TIPS:
Mix even parts of Green acrylic paint and glazing medium. Use a soft cloth to wipe paint on sides, back, front and inside of box.

BUSTILLO

REINA BELLA

MAKERS DON REY W.J. NEFF & CO.

LYRA

THREE TWINS

"A HOWLING SUCCESS"

ROFELDA

ROFELDA

Cigarros Finos

HAND MADE HAND MADE HAND MADE HAND MADE HAND MADE HAND MADE HAND MADE HAND MADE HAND MADE HAND MADE HAND MADE HAND MADE

DIME BANK

MFG. CO.   P.E.R'S

5/8

"Good Friends"

CIGAR — QUEEN SEAL — MILD QUALITY

BUZZER

BLUE RIBBON

CIGAR AROMAS QUALITY

Cigar Corp'n. PEGGY O'NEAL Peggy O'Neal

GLENMORE

MADE IN BELGIUM

ROCKING-HORSE

IMPREGNATED

AVERAGE 50 CONTENTS

SAFETY-MATCHES

BLUE SEAL

LORD STIRLING

MAKERS M.C.C.CO.

BELGIAN MAKE

CROWN POINT

AVERAGE 40 CONTENTS

FINEST QUALITY

PARAFFIN MATCHES

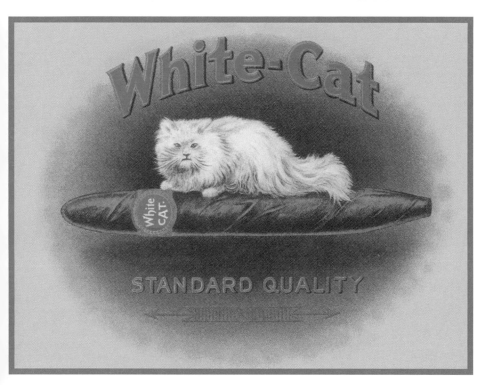

White-Cat

White CAT.

STANDARD QUALITY

IMPREGNATED SAFETY MATCH

DAMP PROOF

AVERAGE 50 STICKS

THE CAMELLIA

MADE IN FINLAND

"LARKSPUR"

BEST QUALITY

Safety Match

AVERAGE CONTENTS 45 · FOREIGN MAKE

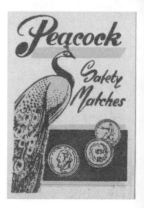

Dogs... Man's Best Friends

This purse is a dog lover's dream come true. These labels offer a wide array of embellishment possibilities. Notice the heart-shaped dog tag. Use your favorite charms, and turn your creativity loose. You may even add a photo of your favorite furry friend.

MATERIALS:

• *Darice* Purse parts (5⅜" x 8½" Wood box, 2 Brass 1¼" handle clamps, Brass 6½" x 5" handle frame, Brass 1" clasp set, 8 Brass corners, 12 Antique Gold 25.5 x11 mm faceted bicone beads, 11 Antique Gold 10.5 mm corrugated rings

• Cigar box labels (Little Doggies, Rover, 8 Gold and Red cigar box borders) • *Design Originals* Legacy Collage Dictionary paper #0547

• *Jesse James* charms (Silver ½" and Gold 1" heart, Gold 1½" hand) • *Westrim* 2" small Silver chain • 18" of Red sequins-by-the-yard

• *DecoArt* (Ivory and Burnt Umber acrylic paint, Satin water based varnish, Matte Clear acrylic sealer) • Adhesives

• Old toothbrush • Craft stick

TIPS:

Paint the sides, back and inside of box with Ivory. Dip toothbrush in Burnt Umber paint thinned with water. Hold brush over box while drawing a craft stick across the bristles.

Brass hand charm

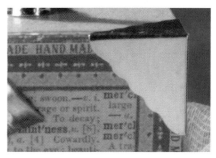

Metal corner

Chain heart

Sequin trim

- Generally wood craft boxes are sturdier and easier to work on than 'true' cigar boxes.
- 'True' Cigar boxes can be purchased on the internet, at flea markets or at tobacco stores. The best source is a cigar aficionado who will donate his boxes to the cause!
- Boxes can be painted, collaged and covered. A minimum of collage and decoration can be quite elegant.
- A game piece closure can be decorated or collaged.
- Torn or ripped edges will add to the arty look of collage pieces.

Game Pieces • Dominoes • Dice • Checkers • Glass Marbles   Tassel   Game Piece Closure   Hardware Clasp

Basic Decoupage Cigar Box

by Robbie Dyess

MATERIALS:
- Wooden box or cigar box
- Plain manila paper • *Judikins* Poly Paper
- Cardboard or chipboard for liner base
- Rubber stamps (*Hampton Art Stamps, Stampers Anonymous, Stampington & Company, A la Art, Limited Edition*) • Black or Brown archival stamp pad • Pigment or dye ink pads
- Thin, workable lining fabric such as cotton or blends • Collage materials (various papers, stamped images, magazine images)
- Metal handle • 8" of thin leather for latch
- Bead or game piece • Embellishments (game pieces, dominoes, letter tiles, glass marbles, tassels)
- Acrylic paint • *Krylon* Workable Fixative • *Judikins* Diamond Glaze • *Mod Podge*
- Craft knife • Ruler or straight edge • Cutting mat • Drill • Metallic leafing pen • Painter's masking tape • *UHU* glue stick • *E6000* glue • White glue

TIPS:

Cut 1½" to 2" wide strip of Poly Paper and adhere with White craft glue to reinforce hinge area of box. Score along hinge seam. Let dry thoroughly. Using acrylic paint or leafing pen, paint inside edges that will not be covered with lining.

Using Mod Podge, decorate outside and inside box lid. Use archival ink to stamp manila paper and create collage pieces. Make sure collage is oriented correctly so that it is in the right direction when box is standing or being carried!

Sponge on added color with pigment or dye inks and acrylic paint after collage is complete.

Measure and drill holes for metal handle and attach with screws. Ends of screws will need to be cut off with heavy duty bolt cutters or rotary tool with cutting disk. Carefully remove handle and screws and set aside.

Measure inside of box by setting it on a piece of lightweight cardboard and trace around box. Using craft knife, cutting mat and straight edge, cut cardboard to fit inside bottom of box. Work slowly to make it fit rather than making large cuts. It is a good idea to make a paper pattern and then cut cardboard. Make cardboard liner pieces to fit sides, top and bottom of box. Cover with fabric or paper using UHU glue, mitering corners of fabric for easy folding.

After bottom liner is in place, add liner pieces to sides of box. Remember, covering cardboard with paper or fabric will change how it fits, so double-check each piece before covering and adhering with glue. After adding liner to top of box, drill a hole in center of handle area for leather cord closure. Drill through liner also.

Using E6000, glue game piece to lid or side of box for closure. Make loop of leather cord and run through hole in handle portion of box, knot on inside to fit game piece.

Reattach metal handle. If cord knot is left exposed, it can easily be adjusted or changed later. Embellish box with dominoes, checkers or dice for feet. Add game pieces beads, charms, etc. with E-6000.

With painter's masking tape, mask off metal handle and any embellishments you do not want glazed or sprayed. If desired, spray entire box with fixative before finishing outside with Diamond Glaze.

Unscrew handle slightly, place tassel under screw, tighten.

If you like unique purses and have trouble finding designs that suit your taste, fashion your own from a cigar box. Use a sturdy wood box then decorate it to suit your heart's desire.

The results are stunning!

1. Reinforce box hinge with Poly Paper strip.

2. Cut decorative paper to fit the box.

3. Stamp images on paper.

4. Gather collage elements and embellishments.

- Metal hinges will extend the life of the box if it is to be repeatedly opened and closed. Remember that long screws will need to be cut off after attaching hinges.
- Add decorative cord around the edges of the inside liner pieces.

5. Collage paper to outside of box.

6. Glue collage elements in place.

7. Drill holes for handle.

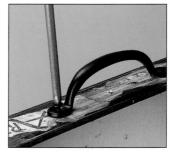

8. Screw handle in place. Remove and set aside.

Basic Collage Cigar Boxes

by Joy Hatcher

A wood box is a functional box with a clasp that a little imagination can transform into a fun, artsy purse.

MATERIALS:

• Wooden box or cigar box
• Decorative paper, photos or die-cuts • Handle (drawer pull, beaded wire, chain or wooden handle used for teapots)
• Embellishments (charms, tags, die-cuts, rhinestones, game pieces, cards, wood shapes, jewelry, coins, buttons, flat glass marbles, fibers, key chains)
• *DecoArt* (acrylic paint, Satin water based varnish)• Sponge brush • Drill with a small bit • Adhesives

TIPS:

Using a sponge brush and acrylic paint, paint one side of box. Work on one side of the box at a time. Quickly apply paint to back of paper, photos or die cuts and press on the prepared side with fingers. Smooth out any wrinkles and bubbles as you work.

Apply a coat of varnish over all artwork, one side at a time. Let each side dry about 30 minutes before turning box over. You may apply additional coats of varnish for a finished look. Allow ample drying time.

Drill holes for handle and insert wire or screws. Attach hinges and clasps.

Glue most embellishments with Goop. Glue lighter weight embellishments with diluted Tacky glue. Add beaded fibers, key chains and tags to handle if desired.

9. Line bottom, sides with fabric covered cardboard.

10. Attach leather loop and game piece for closure.

11. Add a coat of Diamond Glaze to finish purse.

Create your own Artistic Cigar Box for a Purse or Gift!

Red Shoes

Red shoes were popular long before Dorothy wore ruby slippers. Create a jewelry box or sewing case with these fun motifs.

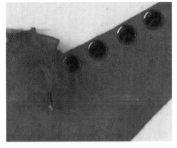

Needle and thread

Ribbon puff and brads

Spool and thimble

Button trim

Flea market buckle

Ribbon bow

MATERIALS:
- *Darice Inc.* 11½" x 8½" wood box
- Cigar box labels (8 Black - Red box borders, 4 Cigar bands)
- *Jesse James* (Silver ⅝" thimble button • Silver 1¾" needle charm • *Offray* (1 Red ¾" ribbon flower, 18" Red ⅜" wide ribbon) • Fabric (8½" x 11½" unbleached muslin, 2 Red prints and 1 Purple print for shoes) • 7" Red 1½" wide grosgrain ribbon • *DMC* #666 Red cotton crochet thread • 1½" x 2" Rhinestone buckle • 4 Silver and Purple beads • 9 Purple iron-on dots • *Lara's Crafts* (4 wood 1¼" balls for feet, 1" wood spool) • 1 sheets of heavy 8½" x 11" cardstock
- *DecoArt* (Red acrylic paint, Satin water based varnish, Matte Clear acrylic sealer) • Adhesives

TIPS:
Paint sides, bottom and inside of box with Red. Paint wood balls Red. • Glue balls to bottom of box. Glue cigar bands to balls. • Varnish box and balls. Let dry. • Apply PEELnSTICK to Red and Purple print fabrics. Cut out shoes. Remove backing from PEELnSTICK and press shoes onto unbleached muslin. Use PEELnSTICK to attach muslin to cardstock and cardstock to box top. • Cut wood spool in half. Wrap Red thread around one half of spool.

Red Hats

Red Hat Ladies are bold, independent, creative, and unique individuals. Express your Red Hat attitude with this purse decorated in bright red, black, and gold.

MATERIALS:
• *Darice* Purse parts (11½" x 8½" wood box, 2 Brass 1¼" handle clamps, Brass 6½" x 5" handle frame, Brass 1" clasp set, 6 Red seed beads • 6 Red 5 mm sequins)
• Cigar box labels (Cigarros Finos, 8 Black and Red cigar box borders)
• 2 *Offray* Red ribbon flowers • 24" of Red metallic braid • *EK Success* typewriter stickers • *Jesse James* (4 Antique Gold corners, 1 Gold 1⅝" filigree square, 1 Gold ⅝" heart button, 1 Gold ¼" star, 1 Gold and Black 1¼" cameo charm) • 4 *Laura's Crafts* wood ⅜" button plugs for feet • Black cardstock
• *DecoArt* (Raw Sienna and Red acrylic paint, Satin water based varnish, Glazing medium) • Adhesives

TIPS:
Thin Raw Sienna paint with water. Use a soft cloth to wipe paint onto sides, front, back and inside box. • Cut a 2½" square of cardstock. Cut notches along one edge forming a combing device. Mix equal parts of Red paint and glazing medium. Paint glaze over stained box front. Draw comb through glaze making wavy lines. • Mat cigar label on Black cardstock. Glue Red metallic braid around label.

Ribbon puffs

Beaded necklace

Metal corner

Cameo charm

Delores Frantz

Delores loves sharing fresh ideas for handmade gifts with people, especially groups of children and adults. This self-taught artist got her start teaching crafts to Girl Scout troops for service projects. Her first publication gave instructions to Girl Scout troop leaders showing how to present simple, inexpensive crafts to their troops.

Delores credits her mother with teaching her to sew and encouraging her to pursue art. Her mom was a professional milliner who loved to sew decorations for the holidays. She carries on this tradition today.

Delores is a multi-talented craft designer and has written many books for Design Originals.

SUPPLIERS - Most craft and variety stores carry an excellent assortment of supplies. If you need something special, ask your local store to contact the following companies:

CIGAR BOX LABELS, DECORATIVE PAPERS
  Design Originals, 800-877-7820, Fort Worth, TX
  www.d-originals.com

WOOD PURSE BOXES, PURSE HARDWARE, BEADS, CHARMS, RHINESTONES
  Darice Inc., 800-321-1494, Strongsville, OH

ACRYLIC PAINT, VARNISH, SEALER, GLAZING
  DecoArt, 800-367-3047, Stanford, KY

PEELnSTICK ADHESIVE
  Therm-O-Web, 800-323-0799, Wheeling, IL

EMBELLISHMENTS
  EK Success, 800-524-1349, Clifton, NJ
  Jesse James Button and Trim,
  610-435-7899, Allentown, PA
  Li'l Davis Designs, 949-838-0344, Irvine, CA
  Making Memories, 801-294-0430, Centerville, UT

WOOD BUTTONS, BALLS, PIECES
  Lara's Crafts, 817-581-5210, Ft Worth, TX

RIBBON
  Offray, 800-344-5533, Hagerstown, MD

MANY THANKS to my friends for their cheerful help and wonderful ideas!
Kathy McMillan • Jennifer Laughlin
Donna Kinsey
David & Donna Thomason

Doll Perfecto

MATERIALS:
• *Darice Inc.* Purse parts (8¼" Square wood box, 2 Silver 1¼" handle clamps, Silver 6½" x 5" handle frame, Silver 1" clasp set, 2 Silver 10.5 mm corrugated rings, 34 Silver 10 mm melon beads)
• Cigar box labels (Dick Custer, Doll Perfecto, 4 cigar bands, 8 Black and Red cigar box borders)
• *Axelrod* Silver stars (Two 1½", Six 1") • Brown craft paper
• *DecoArt* (Burnt Umber acrylic paint, Satin water base varnish, Matte Clear acrylic sealer) • Adhesives

TIPS:
Tear Brown craft paper in small pieces. • Working with one piece at a time, dip into slightly thinned White glue. Position and smooth pieces on purse. Overlap edges covering purse front completely. • When dry, lightly brush thinned Burnt Umber acrylic paint over purse front.

Cats

MATERIALS:
• *Darice Inc.* Purse parts (7½" x 4⅜" wood box, 1 Antique Silver pull handle set, Silver 1" clasp set, 33 assorted Red, Aqua and Crystal rhinestones)
• Cigar box labels (Our Kitties, White Cat, 4 matchboxes, 8 Gold and Red cigar box borders)
• 2 sheets *Design Originals* Legacy Collage TeaDye Script paper #0550
• *Jesse James* (5 Antique Silver rose buttons)
• *DecoArt* (Ivory acrylic paint, Satin water based varnish, Matte Clear acrylic sealer) • Adhesives

TIPS:
Drill two ³⁄₁₆" holes in lid for handle. • Paint the edges and inside of box with Ivory. • Apply PEELnSTICK to the wrong side of the Script paper. Cut 2 pieces of paper to fit the sides of the lid plus ½". Apply paper around sides of lid matching bottom of paper to lip of lid and leaving ½" extending above lid. Fold the ½ of paper over the top edge of box. Cut narrow slashes on rounded edges to make the paper lay flat. Trace around the box top and cut paper to fit the lid. Use this technique to cover the lower portion of the box.

Giraffes

MATERIALS:
• *Darice* Purse parts (11½" x 8½" wood box, 2 Brass 1¼" handle clamps, Brass 6½" x 5" handle frame, Brass 1" clasp set, Assorted Antique Gold beads)
• 8 Gold and Red cigar box borders
• 12" Fabric panel • 6" of Black yarn • 4 Red 10 mm sequins • Seed beads (4 Red, 2 Black, 150 Gold) • 36" Gold sequins-by-the-yard • 4 *Lara's Crafts* wood ⅜" button plugs for feet • Heavy cardstock
• *DecoArt* (Raw Sienna acrylic paint, Satin water based varnish, Matte Clear acrylic sealer) • Adhesive

TIPS:
Use a soft cloth to wipe sides, back and inside of box with Raw Sienna paint thinned with water. Cut heavy cardstock to fit front of box. Use PEELnSTICK to attach fabric to cardstock and cardstock to purse front. Glue beads to fabric.

Star embellishments

Corner trim

jewels

Flower charms

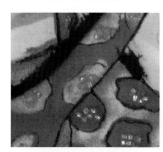

Beaded details

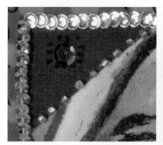

Sequin trim